ISTANBUL

72 Hours in Istanbul

A smart swift guide to delicious food, great rooms and what to do in Istanbul, Turkey.

TRIP PLANNER GUIDES

Copyright © 2015 Trip Planner Guides

All rights reserved. No part of this book may be reproduced in any form or by any electronic or mechanical means including information storage and retrieval systems – except in the case of brief quotations in articles or reviews – without the permission in writing from its publisher.

Although the author and publisher have made every effort to ensure that the information in this book was correct at press time, the author and publisher do not assume and hereby disclaim any liability to any party for any loss, damage, or disruption caused by errors or omissions, whether such errors or omissions result from negligence, accident, or any other cause.

ISBN-13: 978-1517122386

ISBN-10: 1517122384

"If the earth were a single state, Istanbul would be its capital." - Napoleon Bonaparte

TABLE OF CONTENTS

	Before You Get Started…	7
1	Welcome to Istanbul	9
2	Overview of Istanbul Neighborhoods	20
3	Daily Itinerary Planner	32
4	Day One Tour: The Ultimate Introduction To Istanbul	34
5	Day Two Tour: A Day Filled With History, Culture…And A Wee Bit Of Shopping	44
6	Best Istanbul Experiences for Day Three	52
7	An Exciting Night of Entertainment in Istanbul	55
8	Flavors of the Local Cuisine	61
9	Dining in Istanbul	66
10	Istanbul Accommodation Guide	71
11	Istanbul Travel Essentials	78
12	Turkish Language Essentials	81
13	Conclusion	96

BEFORE YOU GET STARTED

We've put together a quick set of tips for maximizing the information provided in this guide.

Insider tips: Found in italics throughout the guide, these are golden nuggets of information picked up during our travels. Use these handy tips to save money, skip the queues and uncover hidden gems.

Maps: This guide connects you to the most up-to-date city and transport maps. Step-by-step instructions are included on how to access. We highly recommend reviewing these maps PRIOR to departing on your trip.

Itineraries: While we have enclosed memorable itineraries for your use, we understand that sometimes you just want to venture out on your own. That is why all major attractions, hotels, restaurants and entertainment venues are tagged with the neighborhood that houses them. In doing so, you'll know what's nearby when planning your adventures.

Budget: Prices at time of publication are provided for all major attractions and a pricing scale is provided for all hotels, restaurants and entertainment.

Websites: To ensure you have the most up-to-date information prior to departure we have included links to venue websites for your convenience. Simply enter the url into your favorite browser to load the webpage.

1 WELCOME TO ISTANBUL

"Istanbul, a universal beauty where poet and archeologist, diplomat and merchant, princess and sailor, northerner and westerner screams with same admiration. The whole world thinks that this city is the most beautiful place on earth."

Edmondo De Amicis

Italian poetic novelist De Amicis may have fallen head over heels in love with 19th century Istanbul, yet if anything can be said of this intoxicating city, is that it really hasn't changed much in the last 100 years. Renowned as the epitome fusion capital of East and West, Istanbul is a cacophony of sights, sounds and smells; an almost chimerical concoction of cultures and religions, which will either leave you salivating for more…or have you running for the exit.

Istanbul is not for the faint-hearted traveler or one who prefers a classic beauty rather than a rough treasure. The sensory overload for which this city is so revered, is not overly kind to the uninitiated. The chaotic flurry of the city's most historic core, brimming with Turkish, Ottoman, Roman, Greek and Byzantine architecture; coupled with insane traffic, maddening crowds and blaring calls to prayer at first light, are just a few of the reasons why Istanbul is often dubbed the most mesmerizing European capital of all. There's no city in the entire continent which can hope to offer the kind of authentic cultural experiences that Istanbul offers at every turn.

This is a place where vertiginous skyscrapers stand alongside century-old bazaars, where traders have been gathering for over a millennia. Where grandiose mosques built by Sultans with more gold than sense still stand proud and loud, and where trendy young teenagers rub shoulders with veiled women of fervent faith. If you prefer to *feel* a world where old meets new, rather than just admire it behind a polished façade, then you'll feel right at home.

Looking for an utterly unique and unforgettable destination for your next getaway?

Let us introduce you to Istanbul.

A Brief Look Back In Time

Thanks to its unique geographical location, the city of Istanbul has been settled, and contested, since ancient times. Many historians believe that its first inhabitants settled in the area as early as the Neolithic period. In 2008, a construction project for a subway station led to the discovery of the area's earliest traces of human settlement, dating back to 6,700 BC.

Istanbul has undergone several name changes throughout its history, due to its inclusion in several different empires of famed note. In the 7th century, King Byzas took his Greek colonists in this area, to establish Byzantium, a colony named after him. King Byzas chose this area after Delphi's oracle told him to settle on the "land of the blind." Legend has it that the Greek king believed that the land's earlier settlers were blind for overlooking a superb land with an excellent location.

Persians ruled the city in the next century. But in the 4th century BC, Alexander the Great conquered the Persians and took over the city. The city became a peaceful haven until the second century BC.

Septimus Severus, a Roman emperor, subjugated Byzantium in 193 AD. The city remained under the rule of the Romans for over 200 years. In 4th century AD, Emperor Constantine the Great changed the city's name to Constantinople and made it the capital of the Roman Empire after defeating Licinius 1, the eastern Roman emperor.

As the capital city of the entire Roman Empire, Constantinople prospered and grew. But in 395, in the wake of Emperor Theodosius's death, a tremendous revolt took place, as his sons divided the empire permanently. In the 400s, the city became the Byzantine Empire's capital.

Early leaders of the Byzantine Empire filled the city with jewels of the ancient world. In the 6th century, the city entered a golden age and took its place as one the great cities of the world. Emperor Justinian built a couple of eye-catching architectural structures, namely the **Sunken Cistern** and **Hagia Sophia**. In addition, he occupied much of southern Europe and northern Africa.

The city's later history, though, is filled with sieges and intrigues. From the 7th to 8th centuries AD, the Arabs besieged the entire city of Istanbul. Also, in the 9th and 10th centuries, the Barbarians attacked this Turkish city. For a while, it was even managed by the Fourth Crusade's members after it was destroyed in 1204.

Led by Sultan Mehmet II, the Ottoman Turks conquered the city in 1453. Eventually, it became the Ottoman Empire's capital city and was renamed to Islambol. During the Ottoman rule, sultans built a legion of public buildings and mosques. In the midst of the 16th century, the city was an epicenter of politics, culture and commerce.

The Ottoman rule lasted until the First World War, when the city was settled by the allied troops. Led by Mustafa Kemal Ataturk, the Turkish nationalists successfully won a war of independence, establishing a new nation called the Republic of Turkey. After the successful war, the capital city was moved from Istanbul to Ankara.

Climate

Istanbul is blessed with a moderate continental temperature, with wet, cold and sporadically snowy winters as well as humid, hot summers. Summertime and late spring are the driest times while winter and late autumn are the wettest.

Istanbul is also one of the very few cities the world with microclimates, thanks to its maritime location, diverse topography and size. As a tourist in this diverse land, you can experience a variety of climates from different regions in just a few days' travel. The Bosporus coastline, as well as the city's northern half, exhibits characteristics of a humid subtropical and ocean climate, because of its lush vegetation and the Black Sea's humidity. Istanbul's southern half, on the other hand, is a bit drier and warmer as well as less affected by the Black Sea's humidity. The eastern part has as continental Anatolian climate while the West has a Balkan environment.

Useful Info at a Glance:

Average Annual Climate: 56.6 degrees Fahrenheit (13.7 degrees Celsius)

Average days of snow: 7

Autumn: September, October and November - 65 degrees F (18 degrees C)

Crisp, clear air and lots of sunshine – prices & crowds drop

Special events (Istanbul Biennial and Contemporary Istanbul)

Winter: December, January & February - 50 degrees F (10 degrees C)

Cold & overcast, but with lowest crowds & prices

Spring: March, April, May – 70 degrees F (21 degrees C)

Stunning! Warm but not hot, the city blooms with color, plethora of festivals is held!

Summer: June, July, August & September - 70s-80 degrees F (24-27 degrees C)

Exceptionally hot in July, swollen crowd & prices are at their peak

Languages

Turkish is the most prevalent language in the city and Kurdish is spoken by a large number of Instanbul-ites. English speakers won't have to worry about the language barrier too much, as capital city inhabitants, under the age of 40, are pretty fluent in English.

Getting in

Getting to the city of Istanbul is rather easy, and can be done in a variety of ways. After all, the city is home to a couple of international airport and two bus stations, where international services depart and arrive. In addition, it has a pair of international train stations to boot.

Istanbul Ataturk Airport: the city's main aviation hub caters to over 19 million passengers every year and is serviced by a plethora of international airlines, including Tunisiar, Turkish Airlines, Etihad Airways, and Emirates.

http://www.ataturkairport.com/en-EN/Pages/Main.aspx

Sabiha Gokcen Airport: the city's second hub, is nestled on Istanbul's Asian side. This airport is primarily used to cater local flights, as well as budget airlines, some of which connect passengers to international destinations like Budapest, Amsterdam, and Doha.

http://www.sabihagokcen.aero/homepage

Sirkeci Train Terminal: Passengers from two different European destinations arrive at Sirkeci Train Terminal on a daily basis. The Balkan Express transports travelers from Belgrade to Sirkeci via Bulgaria's Sofia. The Bosphorous Express, meanwhile, departs from Bucharest and conveys passengers to the Sirkeci Terminal.

http://www.tcdd.gov.tr/tcdding/

Ferry services: There are international ferries that transport tourists from Italy, Ukraine, Russia, Libya, and Greece. For the most part, these ferries stop at the Karakoy Port, which is located near Taksim and Sultanahmet. From Karakoy Port, you can take a cruise ship that docks close to the city's downtown area. Furthermore, there are taxi cabs at the port's entrance that offer rides to various locations in the city.

http://www.turkeylogue.com/ferries.html

Esenler Otogar Bus Depot: Most long-haul coaches terminate at the colossal Esenler Otogar, nestled on the city's European side. Here, buses arrive and depart for all regions of the country as well as for international destinations like Romania, The Republic of Macedonia, Greece, and Bulgaria.

Reaching Istanbul by car is certainly not for the faint-hearted, as the city centre's traffic is insanely congested. If overlanding, we recommend you park and store your vehicle at least 10 to 20kms outside of Istanbul, and reach the city by public transport from there. A special permit and payable fees are required to drive on the highway and cross the Bosphorus bridges.

Getting around

Do you have an adventurous soul? If your answer is a 'yes', then explore the city on foot. As a tourist, walking can be an easy and pleasurable way to discover the city's colorful bazaars, stunning alleys, and some of its hidden gems. What's more, walking gives you a taste of everyday life in Istanbul.

Dolmuses: If you are planning on traveling greater distances, or staying in one of the city's outer suburbs, you will need to get acquainted with the city's buses. Unlike what you may be used to, buses in Istanbul are tiny. They're essentially mini-vans, or people-movers, which have been turned into public modes of transport. *Dolmuses*, as these buses are called, are plentiful and inexpensive to ride although you will have to know 1) Where you're going, 2) Which number dolmus to take, and 3) where you should get off. Get all this info from your hotel concierge before you leave for the day and have a map ready.

Trams: Are also an ideal means of transportation, as you explore the city of Istanbul. Not only are they fast, but they provide astounding cityscape sights as well. The Zeytinburnu-Kabatas Tram is arguably the best for alighting at the most sought-after attractions in the city.

Metro: Please note that due to the high concentration of historic sites in the centre, Istanbul's Metro is quite a useless mode of transport for sightseeing, and is only convenient when heading to/from the airport.

Water ferries: Depart from the city's Asian and European sides. As you take a ferry ride to the city, you get a chance to see the beauty of Istanbul from a completely different perspective.

Taxis: Cabs are quite abundant in this vibrant metropolis, yet although they are convenient and cheap, they aren't necessarily your best option. Taxi drivers here have a reputation of being opportunistic to say the least. Nonetheless, a taxi can come in hand, especially in the evening.

Istanbul Tourist Pass: As a tourist, you should consider investing in a Tourist Pass, which grants you huge discounts on all public transport rides, as well as free entry into 20 or so of the city's attractions.

http://www.istanbultouristpass.com

Insider's Tip: The Tourist Pass is definitely a worthwhile investment if you plan to visit a lot of attractions, and have an aversion to queues. Even IF it were to save you no money at all, getting fast-tracked through the queues would make it worthwhile enough, yet the monetary value is also very good. Hint: order this before you arrive and have it sent to your hotel so it'll be there when you arrive!

Istanbul Museum Pass: The only tourist oriented card aimed at facilitating and combining all your sightseeing activities. The Museum Pass is valid for 5 days (120 hours) and costs 85 TL. The card allows for free entry into about a dozen famous sights, including Hagia Sofia and Topkapı, among quite a few minor landmarks. Moreover it allows for quite big discounts on all other attractions, landmarks and museum. Is it worth it? Again, for the price, you'd need to visit Topkapı, Hagia Sofia and at least three other museums or attractions, to make it worth your monetary value. Having said this, skipping the queues (once again) is the most important convenience of this card.

http://museumpassistanbuldistributor.com/2012/05/09/museum-pass-istanbul/

2 OVERVIEW OF ISTANBUL NEIGHBORHOODS - HOW NOT TO GET LOST

Istanbul is a sprawling, busy metropolis of 14 million people. For first-time visitors, this can be insanely overwhelming.

Where would one even start?

A good understanding of the city's layout is imperative if you wish to make the most of your visit, as is getting to grips with the public transport. This is, perhaps, the most important point.

Insider's Tip: When choosing a base point, like in many large capitals the world over, it's wise to look at a particular suburb's connection to the centre by public transport, rather than its geographical proximity to it. It's all well and good that X is closer to the centre, but if it's not well service by buses, dolmuşes (mini vans) or trains then you're better off staying in Y, even if it's a little further away. You with us so far? Great!

Overview

Istanbul is divided in two parts, a European side on the West and Asian side on the East, connected over the Bosphorus Strait by the very impressive,

Bosphorus Bridge. All of the main historical attractions are on the European side of the Strait and this is where we'd recommend you stay if it is your first time visiting. The Asian side is actually gorgeous and much more peaceful (and a little cheaper too) although because it requires a little more confidence in minibus hopping, staying here is preferred by return visitors. Perhaps something you could keep in mind for your second visit to Istanbul!

Insider's tip: Do note that local Instanbul-ites are exceptionally friendly and helpful to foreign visitors, even when they're not trying to sell them something. Don't be afraid to ask for assistance or directions should you need to. English is spoken very well by anyone under 50 years of age, generally speaking.

Here's our overview of Istanbul's most popular suburbs. **For greater convenience, we will refer to these suburbs when mentioning activities, eating and shopping options.**

Sultanahmet – The Historic Centre

Sultanahmet is the historic core of Istanbul and boasts the city's major highlights. Historically, this part of town was known as Constantinople, a former city of the Roman Empire. Sultanahmet is a compact maze of cobblestone alleyways, brimming with exotic bazaars, grandiose palaces and opulent mosques. It lies in-between the Bosphorus, the

Golden Horn and the Sea of Marmara. Visitors flock to this neighborhood to explore the Topkapi Palace, a symbol of Istanbul's royal past and the former home of ancient rulers. Around the same block, you will also find the Archaeology Museum, which is home to the city's historic artifacts from the Mesopotamians and Ottomans, to Alexander the Great. The much revered Hagia Sophia is here, as is the Grand Bazaar, one of the oldest trading bazaars in the world.

Sultanahmet is best serviced by tramline T1 although a myriad of minibuses reach this centre from all over Istanbul.

Insider's tip: If you are only visiting for a couple of days, we highly recommend you search accommodation in this area, thus avoiding any need for tram, bus or taxi rides, except to and from the airport. Public transportation in Istanbul is surprisingly easy to use, but is quite time consuming.

Beyoğlu – Hip and Happening Heart of Istanbul

Beyoğlu could be said to be an extension of Sultanahmet, and is usually the first place visitors will head to, once they eventually emerge from Sultanahmet. This is the commercial and entertainment quarter of the city, and where you'll find infamous Taksim Square, the Istiklal shopping strip, Galata Tower, the amazing Modern Art Museum and an array of cultural highlights including Catholic Churches, Jewish Synagogues and, of course, plenty of mosques. Cool and trendy restaurants, cafés and boutiques make this the busiest – and buzziest – part of Istanbul. If you want to immerse yourself in that fusion of West, East, Old and New, then Beyoğlu will do you well.

Insider tip: Travelling alone but like to go out at night? Stay here! Beyoglu is the part of Istanbul which most resembles New York, where life is vibrant 24/7 and there's always something to see, do and eat after the sun has set. In Beyoglu, the action will be on right outside your front door. Sultanahmet, after dinner, is a lot more subdued, which suits families and older travelers much more than young backpackers.

New City – The Flashy Business Quarter

If you were to simply walk north from Taksim Square, you would eventually end up in New City. Standing in stark contrast to Sultanahmet, New City is a maze of vertiginous and flashy skyscrapers, top-class hotels, clubs, bars and restaurants. The suburbs of Kurtuluş, and Şişli, Elmadağ, and Nişantaşı, are all found here. This is where the fascinating Ataturk Museum is found, dedicated to the father of modern-day Turkey.

Insider's tip: This quarter is characterized by glitzy malls, glass skyscrapers and trendy cafés, which is great if you've been in Turkey for months but not necessarily entertaining or mesmerizing if you're on a week-long vacation. Aside the Ataturk Museum – which is immensely interesting – most tourists find very little reason to spend much time here. This is the side of Istanbul which looks like every other European city!

The Bosphorus – Istanbul's Revered Natural Landmark

The Bosphorus Straight is one of the world's largest waterways, which connects the Black Sea with the Sea of Marmara. The scenery of this area is truly breathtaking, most especially at sunset and from the comfort of a boat. The shores are lined with tiny villages, ruins, palaces and Turkey's beloved tea gardens. It is no surprise that the most luxurious hotels in Istanbul are located in this area, as the coastal views are out of this world!

From the Marmara Tram Station, visitors can connect to different neighborhoods within the city. However, the quickest way to get around the Bosphorus and to the Prince's Islands specifically is by Ferry F1. Take tram T1 to Eminönü to access the ferry docks.

Insider's Tip; Along the waterside promenade you'll come across a plethora of tour boats offering 'sightseeing cruises' starting at about $20 per person. A most rewarding and infinitely cheaper way to cruise the Bosphorus is to hop on one of the commuter ferries instead. You can enjoy an hour-long ride, stopping along the way and admiring all *the shoreline attractions (like the stupendous Dolmabahçe Palace), minus the annoying and hard to understand commentary of the tour boats AND at about a quarter of the price. Bliss!*

Prince's Islands – An Oasis in the City

This archipelago of nine islands make up the Adalar quarter of Istanbul and visiting is about the only full-day activity Istanbul has to offer from its centre. This is where locals escape to on a weekend, to have a break from the ever-bustling city. These islands are like an oasis in the heart of crazy Istanbul, where all motorized transport banned and replaced by bicycles and horse-drawn carriages. This is an extremely charming place to explore at length, with not much to do other than strolling along the sea shores and enjoying romantic picnics under the trees. Only four of the islands are accessible to visitors, namely, Burgazada, Heybeliada, Kınalıada *and* Büyükada, the last being the largest and most popular where you can visit the historic Greek Monastery of St George. The hard 20-minute uphill hike is definitely a worthwhile activity. To reach the Prince's Islands catch Ferry F1 from the Bosphorus dock. There are over fourteen services during the day, starting form 6.30am right up until about 10pm.

Insider's tip: Is it worth dedicating an entire day to Adalar? In short 'yes, definitely' BUT only once you've ticked off the city's main highlights first. Even then, make sure it is not on a week-end.

There is only one true tactic which ensures that you never get (permanently) lost when exploring Istanbul. Sure, you're bound to get disoriented through the endless maze that is Sultanahmet, and more than one visitor has had a tough time finding a way out of the Grand Bazaar. But to be honest, these are sometimes the best ways to discover the true hidden treasures of this city.

Yet heading off into a far corner of the city and getting hopelessly lost at the end of your day is never much fun. So, to this end, we recommend you always carry all the details of your place of accommodation (name address & phone number), as well as detailed maps of the areas you wish to explore.

Useful Maps & General Info

Maps are an invaluable asset for any curious traveler, especially one who wishes to get a little off the beaten path. There are a few elementary factors, however, which you should keep in mind when scouring the net or the book-shop for great maps of Istanbul.

-They must be in both English AND Turkish. Do not assume all locals will be able to read English and thus, be of any help to you.

-They must be recent. Istanbul has been sitting proudly in its spot since time immemorial, yet names of streets and entire suburbs can change, and restaurants and cafés can move. The Blue Mosque may not be 'going anywhere' any time soon, but outdated maps are as useful as non-existent ones.

-Whatever you do, locate, download, print and buy maps BEFORE you travel. The last thing you want to do is waste precious holiday time by sussing out print joints or book stores when already in Istanbul.

Here are some online maps, current at time of writing, which should help you make heads and tails of this wondrous city.

General City Map

The best overview maps online are courtesy of Michelin Maps. Go online here and have a look at the detailed map of Istanbul:

http://tinyurl.com/michelinistanbul

Click on the links up top to denote your desired attractions (hotels, restaurants, tourist attractions and even parking stations. You can calculate driving times and routes between two points, and even click on the weather icon to see the current weather conditions. Once you've zoomed in on your particular area of choice, simply click on the 'share' button, and proceed to 'print'.

Walking Tour of Sultanahmet Map

Take this easy and comprehensive walking tour and you'll stroll for an entire day (if stopping at most sights) and cover about two miles. Click here to see the map and have a look at all the attractions listed

http://tinyurl.com/walkistanbul

and here to actually download the map to your PC

http://tinyurl.com/walkistanbuldownload

GPS MY City App

This fantastic app can be downloaded, stored and used offline when in Istanbul, requiring no internet coverage aboard. Click here to access 16 different walking tours with map

http://tinyurl.com/mycityistanbul

A light version can be downloaded free of charge while a full version is only $4.99 through the App Store.

Transportation Maps

For an overview of all Istanbul's major modes of public transport, click here

http://tinyurl.com/majortransportistanbul

For the Metro network, click here

http://tinyurl.com/metroistanbul

For the Tram network, click here

http://tinyurl.com/tramistanbul

To print any of these maps, simply right-mouse click on map and select 'print'

Official Tourism Website

HowToIstanbul is the city's first official tourism portal and brimming with great info and up-to-date details on what's happening in and around the city, upcoming concerts, shows, events and more.

http://howtoistanbul.com/

There are six Tourist Offices (called *Turist Danışma Ofisi*) located in various areas of Istanbul. All are found on the European side. Officially, they should offer a wealth of information, infinite number of brochures and maps, and an abundance of info in different languages. In reality, however, they often fall short of all those things and are renowned for opening, closing and taking breaks whenever the fancy takes them. This is the reason it is imperative you do most of your research before you even arrive to Istanbul, as although you will get a free (and very good) map of Istanbul in one of these establishments, the staff is not nearly as helpful as, perhaps, they should be.

Nevertheless, these are the addresses and contact details of Tourist Offices.

Atatürk Havalimanı- Ataturk Airport

Atatürk Hava Limanı içi -Yeşilköy

Open from 8am to 11pm, this is a small info booth which you'll see after you pass customs

+90 (212) 465 3151 / 465 3547

Taksim- Hilton Hotel

Elmadağ / Taksim

Open from 8.30am to 5pm, but closes on Sundays

+90 (212) 233 0592

Beyazıt Square

Beyazıt Meydanı

From 8.30am to 6pm

+90 (212) 522 49 02

Karaköy Cruise Ship Terminal

Karaköy Limanı Yolcu Salonu İçi

No confirmed opening times, generally only when ships dock.

+90 (212) 249 57 76

Sirkeci Train Station

Sirkeci Garı

From 9am to 5pm

+90 (212) 511 58 88

Sultanahmet Hippodrome

Meydanı

Open from 9am to 5pm

+90 (212) 518 18 02 / 518 87 54

3 DAILY ITINERARY PLANNER

Is it possible to explore the city's most beloved and remarkable tourist attractions in three days or less? Sure, why not! Harder feats have been accomplished. Question is...is it worth it? The answer to that is a most resounding YES! Even an hour spent in Istanbul, rather than anywhere else, is worth it. However...it pays to keep in mind that your enjoyment of a three-day stopover to Istanbul will be determined by just how much you wish to cram into your days. Think you'll strike off Topkapi Palace, the Blue Mosque and Hagia Sophia in a single day? Keep dreaming! Or maybe not...

Insider's Tip: Istanbul's most revered and famous sites are not only insanely time-consuming to visit, but on a busy summer's day, just queuing to buy tickets and enter can take a couple of hours. When planning to visit one of the above-mentioned three masterpieces, we recommend you not plan anything 'big' to see or do before or after, as you will no doubt be tired, thirsty, hungry and all sighted-out by the time you emerge. A leisurely lunch, stroll by the Bosphorus or spot of shopping ought to be fine activities to combine with a visit here.

First of all, it helps to have a general idea of what

the BIG attractions are in Istanbul, the ones which require a half-day from start to finish (4 hours or so), and ones which can take from half an hour to an hour. Combine one BIG and several smaller attractions in a single day and you're bound to have an enjoyable yet enlightening day.

Here's a general overview of the major highlights in Istanbul:

The BIG ones: Topkapi Palace, Hagia Sophia, Blue Mosque. These are recommended places to visit first thing in the morning.

Next up- still amazing but require less time: Basilica Cistern, Chora Church, Galata Tower, Süleymaniye Mosque, Walls of Constantinople, Dolmabahçe Palace.

Leisure pleasures: Grand Bazaar and Spice Bazaar, Bosphorus cruise, strolling through Istiklal Caddesi to Taksim Square, Istanbul Sapphire observation deck, hammam (Turkish baths), eating, drinking and clubbing. Culture shows, Istanbul Sapphire Observation Deck.

On first glance you can see that it is in fact possible to do quite a lot, even in just three days. The bad news is that you won't end up ticking all the items on your list, and the good news…is that you won't end up ticking all the items on your list!

The best part about Istanbul is that you can visit 20 times and will still find plenty to see and do.

4 DAY ONE TOUR: THE ULTIMATE INTRODUCTION TO ISTANBUL

Pay homage to the ancient Ottomans at their sublime palace, savor your first authentic doner kebab in Turkey and learn all the tricks of the trade at the Grand Bazaar, after descending into the dark and refreshing depth of the city's most historic cistern. Cap off your day with a luscious session in a local hammam.

What to see: TOPKAPI PALACE

Overview of Activity: The residence of the Sultans of the Ottoman Empire, for four out of the six centuries they ruled over Turkey.

Why you should go: Because it's insanely opulent and filled with priceless religious relics as well as ancient artifacts. The best views over the Bosphorus are actually from the pristine gardens of this palace.

District: Sultanahmet

Directions: Easy to walk to from all points in Sultanahmet, Topkapi is directly behind Hagia Sophia and takes up the whole eastern corner of the historic centre, right along the shores of the Bosphorus.

Address: Gulhane Park

Operating hours: 9 am to 4.45 pm in winter (October to April)

9 am to 6.45 pm in summer

Ticket booths shut 45 minutes before closing time

Phone #: +90 212 512 0480

Reservation Online:
http://www.muze.gov.tr/buy_e_ticket

Cost (in local currency): 30 TL

Suggested arrival time & duration: Get here 20 minutes before opening time and, once inside, head straight for the Harem, which is the one place which eventually builds up huge queues. The other two rooms which you'll need to line up for are the Treasury and Chamber of Sacred Relics. You can skip all the queues, but visiting at least one of these rooms first and foremost, will save you much time. Don't be tempted to visit the rooms in a logical sequence, but pick the most famous first, and backtrack if you must, later. This Palace usually takes about 4 hours, and that's when the crowds are not excessive. In high season you can add another hour to that.

Once you emerge overawed from the opulence of Topkapi Palace, you'll probably be quite ravenous!

Take your taste buds over to **Konyali Lokantasi Restaurant**. Although a little on the pricey side, this place boasts magnificent views over the harbor and makes for an unforgettable memory on your first day in Istanbul. The food, service and vistas all view for your praise here. Try the Ottoman doner kebab and order a refreshing home-made Aryan drink to copmplement. Don't forget to order a traditional Turkish coffee after your meal, they make a real event out of serving it!

Where to eat: KONYALI LOKANATSI RESTAURANT

District: Sultanahmet

Directions: You'll find Konyali on the north-eastern corner of Topkapı. Make sure you keep walking 'till the end of the property, because the restaurant is set on the downhill and you (almost) have to walk on top of it to actually see it!

Address: Topkapi Palace

Operating hours: Open for breakfast, lunch & dinner

Phone #: +90 212 513 9696

Cost (in local currency): On the high end of the Istanbul dining spectrum, lunch will set you back about 60 TL per person.

Suggested arrival time & duration: 12.30pm. Lunch should take about an hour, but make that two if you wish to enjoy the views and a very leisurely lunch.

Once you have your energy – and your second wind back, it's time to get a move on. You've got some shopping to do! On your way to the Grand Bazaar, however, stop and admire one of the city's last remaining ancient cisterns.

No trip to the city of Istanbul is complete without a visit to the amazing **Basilica Cistern**, built in 532 CE to provide water to the inhabitants of the city. Located right across the Blue Mosque, this mystical cistern will make you feel like you are stepping back in time. Constructed using plinths, capitals and columns from ruined structures, the cistern's grandeur of conception and symmetry are extraordinary. The cooling air down below is a godsend on a hot day!

What to see: BASILICA CISTERN

Overview of Activity: Descend into one of Istanbul's most historic and impressive sites

Why you should go: Because it's revered as one of the greatest achievements of the Byzantine Empire

District: Sultanahmet (Beyazit side)

Directions: From Topkapi Palace, walk down as if going to Hagia Sofia, and keep to the right hand side of the museum, turn right on Hagia Sofia Street

(Ayasofia Meydani) and the cistern will be on your left hand side, just after the intersection.

Address: Yerebatan Caddesi 13

Operating hours: Open daily from 9 am to 6:30 pm

Phone #: +90 212 522 1259

Cost (in local currency): 10 TL

Website: http://yerebatan.com/homepage/basilica-cistern/about-us.aspx#_=_

Suggested arrival time & duration: After lunch is the quietest time at this site. A visit ought to take no more than half an hour.

Ready to shop yet?

With more than 3,000 shops and 60 covered streets, Istanbul's **Grand Bazaar** is truly one of the world's oldest and largest covered markets. Drawing more than 200,000 visitors daily, this chaotic covered market is a whirlwind of aromatic spices, colorful clothing, traditional souvenirs, glistening jewelry and artistic Turkish carpets. Even if you are not planning on shopping, a visit here will delight due to its buzzing scene and bohemian vibes. As a matter of fact, a visit here allows you to learn more about the city's past and culture. If buying anything, channel your inner eastern trader and bargain for a fair price.

Insider's Tip: When visiting the Grand Bazaar, it's imperative you channel your inner eastern trader and polish those bargaining skills! Rule of thumb is to halve whatever the asking price, and sloooowly bargain up from there. Don't start bargaining for anything you are not seriously interested in, and walk away as a last tactic. Chances are you WILL find your coveted item elsewhere.

What to see: GRAND BAZAAR

Overview of Activity: One of the world's largest – and oldest – covered markets

Why you should go: Because it's an exceptional feast for all your senses

District: Sultanahmet (Beyazit side)

Directions: The Grand Bazaar is attached to the Istanbul University and boasts twenty-six entrances. When coming from the Basilica Cistern, you should approach it from Yeniceriler Caddesi. Don't worry, signs directing you to the Grand Bazaar are scattered all over Sultanahmet!

Address: Beyazit Gate

Operating hours: 9 am to 7 pm from Monday to Saturday

Phone #: +90 212 519 1248

Website:
http://www.grandbazaaristanbul.org/Grand_Bazaar_Istanbul.html

Suggested arrival time & duration: Any visit to the Grand Bazaar will probably not take more than two hours. The chaotic crowds will soon drive you out and it matters not when you choose to visit!

You will surely wish to retreat to your hotel after a visit to the Grand Bazaar. Although you may be tempted to simply jump in a shower to refresh...hold that thought! Go ahead and drop off all that shopping, but head out again for an hour or two of blissful rejuvenation.

A perfect way to end a day your first full day of fun and adventure is to indulge in a soothing Turkish bath, with your family or loved one, at the Suleymaniye Haman. For an affordable price, you can pamper yourself in a sauna as well as calm your senses in a relaxing and intense soap massage. To make your massage more pleasurable, the venue has a calming ambiance and a beautiful interior embellished with intricate marble inlays. What's more, it is a 500 year old historic hamam which boasts dramatic domes and archways. Please note that this is a (semi) tourist oriented hamam, so it is mixed sex but accepts only couples and families. If you're travelling solo, check out our next recommendation listed below.

Insider's Tip: does it all sound a little too relaxing to be true? That's probably because it is. The soak in a hamam may be soothing, yet the scrubbing compliments of big Turkish mamas, is anything but! These ladies will exfoliate you to within an inch of your life and that tan you've been working on? Yep. It will be gone. Once you've had a hamam session, all other spas will simply pale in comparisons. Not for wusses.

What to see: SULEYMAN HAMAM

Overview of Activity: Soak, steam and scrub

Why you should go: Because a Turkish hamam is about the most invigorating treatment you could ever have

District: Suleymaniye

Directions: This hamam is located on the eastern gate of the Suleymaniye Mosque, only 350m from the Vezneciler Metro Stop, and only 650m from the Grand Bazaar Tram Stop

Address: Minar Sinan Cad. No.20, Suleymaniye

Operating hours: 10 am to 11 pm (last entry is at 9pm)

Phone #: +90 212 520 3410

Website: http://www.suleymaniyehamami.com.tr/

Cost (in local currency): 125 TL for 90 minutes of treatment

TRIP PLANNER GUIDES

Suggested arrival time & duration: A visit here will take about 2 hours. Before dinner (say, between 6 pm and 7 pm) is the ideal time to visit, as a hamam is best enjoyed on an empty stomach

Are you a solo traveler who wants to experience a soothing hamam? Then, the Ayasofa Hurrem Sultan Hamam should be your top choice. Housed in A beautiful historic building, this hamam facility not only offers hamam, but also offers a wide range of spa services including back massage, aroma explosion, and many more.

What to see: AYASOFA HURREM SULTAN HAMAM

Overview of Activity: Separated into men's and women's quarters, this authentic experience will definitely shake off any inhibitions you may have. Proceed with gusto!

Why you should go: Because it accepts single travelers AND is as historic and stunning as Suleyman

District: Sultanahmet

Directions: In the heart of the historic district, this hamam in only one block south of Hagia Sofia, on the eastern edge of Sultan Ahmet Park

Address: Cankurtaran Mahallesi Ayasofya Meydani No.2

Operating hours: 8 am to 10 pm

Phone #: +90 212 517 3535

Website: http://www.ayasofyahamami.com/

Cost (in local currency): Treatment costs range from 260 TL to 530 TL depending on treatments/duration of stay

Suggested arrival time & duration: A visit to a hamam is a great idea at any time of day, but always best in between meal times

Insider's Tip: Istanbul is home to a near infinite array of gorgeous hamams which offer entry prices of merely 10 TL, as long as they are not housed within historic buildings. They're not nearly as fancy and the experience not as opulent as the more famous ones; yet if it's an authentic scrub you're after than rest assured they are just as good, if not more so, than the pricier options. Considering a hamam visit is a weekly tradition for most Turks, ask for recommendations from those who don't 'need' to recommend the best places. The best advice on this usually comes from the mouth of cleaning ladies in every hotel in Istanbul, so do tap into this invaluable goldmine of info.

5 DAY TWO TOUR: A DAY FILLED WITH HISTORY, CULTURE…AND A WEE BIT OF SHOPPING

Rise and shine…you're in Istanbul!!

Head off to admire the wonders of **Hagia Sofia Museum** today and, if you can, combine this with a visit to the Blue Mosque, BEFORE HEADING TO Taksim Square and Istiklal Cadesi for some great shopping.

Aya Sofia is a splendid architectural gem, one which is sure to leave you in awe with its imperial beauty and unique design. Built in 537 by Emperor Justinian, this site was once a church, and was later reformed as a mosque in the year 1453. But in 1934, Hagia Sophia was transformed into a world-class museum. Lauded as one of the greatest architectural achievements in the world, this site is popular for its gigantic dome, and gleaming interior made up over 20 million gold tiles. Besides its one-of-a-kind design, the palace also holds a vast amount of mosaics, exhibits, and relics, such as the True Cross's fragments, Jesus' shroud, and many more.

What to see: HAGIA SOFIA MUSEUM

Overview of Activity: The mosque/church/museum is stunning to look at, and home to priceless antique mosaics

Why you should go: Because it is striking beyond words AND it's very cool to be in a building which was one both a mosque and a Christian church

District: Sultanahmet

Directions: Hagia Sofia is the heart and soul of historic Istanbul, found right between Topkapi Palace and Basilica Cistern.

Address: Ayasofia Square

Operating hours: 9 am to 5 pm, from Tuesday to Sunday – open until 7pm in summer - last entry is 1hr before closing time

Phone #: +90 212 522 1750

Website: http://ayasofyamuzesi.gov.tr/

Cost (in local currency): 30 TL

Suggested arrival time & duration: As with all major sites, arrive 15-20 minutes before opening. If you explore every nook of this museum, expect it to take about two hours.

Next on your agenda is the iconic **Blue Mosque**, or also called the Sultan Ahmet Mosque. Built by architect Mehmet Aga, the Blue Mosque was designed to rival and surpass the majestic beauty and grandeur of Aya Sofya. Known for its distinct bluish interior, the mosque has spectacular walls covered in magnificent blue tiles. In addition, it features six minarets and a spacious courtyard that is considered the largest of all the mosques made by the Ottoman Empire.

Can't appreciate the mosque's beauty from the outside? Get inside the complex through the Hippodrome, and not from the Sultanahmet Park. As soon as you reach the courtyard, you will be able to appreciate the perfect proportions and fine details of this Ottoman masterpiece.

What to see: SULTAN AHMET (BLUE) MOSQUE

Overview of Activity: This is the only mosque in Turkey to boast 6 minarets. Intricately and opulently decorated, this thriving mosque offers a respite from the chaos of the city

Why you should go: Because this is, without a doubt, the most beautiful building in Istanbul. A working mosque, it offers an architectural, historical and cultural experience, all bundled into one.

District: Sultanahmet

Directions: The city's most prominent landmark is on the southern end of the historic centre, separated by Hagia Sofia by the gorgeous Sultan Ahmet Park, and one block south of the Sultanahmet metro station.

Address: At Meydanı No: 7

Operating hours: From sunrise to sunset, but note that it is close to non-worshippers during the five daily prayer times

Phone #: +90 212 458 4468

Website: http://www.sultanahmetcami.org/

Cost (in local currency): Free of charge

Suggested arrival time & duration: Outside of prayer time, the mosque is open to the public all day. Do wear respectable clothing which covers shoulders and knees. Women ought to bring a long a scarf or pashmina to cover their heads as they enter.

After a full morning of cultural immersion, it's time to immerse yourself in Istanbul's street food scene. Yesterday you flavored a fancy doner kebab, but today is time you got acquainted with the much more common, popular and beloved version, sold off stalls in just about every street of the city. The infamous doner kebab is a classic Turkish dish made of roasted and shredded lamb or chicken, served in durum bread with onions, tomatoes and lettuce and topped with garlic and hummus sauces. Pick yours up from a stand in Sultanahmet and expect to pay about 8TL.

After lunch, head over to **Istiklal Caddesi**, the most famous commercial street in Istanbul. This crowded cobbled street is the center of the city's life, and a 1.4-kilometer long shopping strip home to a multitude of restaurants, chocolateries, patisseries, night clubs, cafes, libraries, art galleries, theatres, bookstores, music stores, and boutiques of every kind. What's more, the street has a colony of Art Deco buildings as well as Ottoman era architectures designed in Art Nouveau, Beaux-Arts, Renaissance Revival, Neo-Gothic and Neo-Classical styles. It's a mouthful just to read it, imagine what it's like to see it!

Insider's Tip: Feeling hot and bothered in Istanbul? Indulge in the local ice cream, called dondurma, which you'll see sold from street stands all over Istiklal Caddesi. This Turkish ice cream is quite different from your standard ice cream. Not only does it have a distinct nectarous taste, but it also has an elastic, thick and chewy texture. Plus, it never seems to melt! Two to three scoops dondurma typically costs around 2.5 TL.

What to see: ISTIKLAL CADDESI

Overview of Activity: Window (and real) shopping, people watching, eating, coffee and tea drinking

Why you should go: Because it's where the 'cool' people hang out, plus there's a historic tram which runs down the length of it.

District: Beyoğlu

Directions: To reach Istiklal Caddesi, simply hop on the T1 Tram Line from the historic centre, directed towards Kabatas. Get off at Karakoy Station and join the Tunel, the world's third-oldest and shortest underground tram. Merely a minute later you will emerge at Istiklal Caddesi.

Suggested arrival time & duration: There is something happening on this street all day and night long, so no matter when you come you're bound to have a look to admire. Having said this, there's a vast array of patisseries here so whenever you come, come with a sweet tooth!

Insider's Tip: Right at the eastern end of Istiklal Caddesi, is where you'll come to **Taksim Square**, *the reputed 'Times Square' of Istanbul and the focal point of the city's social life. Along with* **Gezi Park** *next door, Taksim Square gained international notoriety a few years back when it was the turned into the headquarters of the Turkish Revolution. Although not nearly as exciting as Times Square, this is a gorgeous part of Istanbul nonetheless, and where the city's uni students come to picnic and hang out. Do the same, bring a take away kebab here, find a nice, shaded spot and absorb the laid-back, youthful atmosphere.*

After spending a most leisurely time in this historic centre, it's time to enjoy something rather spectacular...

Head to the **Istanbul Sapphire**, the tallest skyscraper in the country, and get here in time to watch a spectacular sunset over Istanbul. Rising 54 floors above the ground, the Istanbul Sapphire is a towering figure that dominates the stunning city skyline. This lofty skyscraper is currently one of the top 10 tallest buildings in Europe. A commercial and residential building, the Sapphire boasts a simply stunning rooftop observation deck, which is 238 meters above ground. The uninterrupted sweeping panorama of the entire city is breathtaking to say the least. Aside from the observation deck, you can also try out the cutting-edge 4D helicopter simulator on the 56th floor of the skyscraper. With this high-tech simulator, you get to know exactly how it feels to fly over Istanbul in a helicopter.

What to see: ISTANBUL SAPPHIRE

Overview of Activity: A small but fancy shopping mall AND the best views in town? What more could one ask for…

Why you should go: Because the views are OUT OF THIS WORLD!

District: Levent, the city's business district

Directions: The Sapphire is in Levent, about 8km north of Taksim Square. You could either take a cab or, alternatively, reach it by Metro. There is a stop at Taksim Square and you can catch the metro head to Levent, taking the 4th Levent stop. From here, there are signs which will direct you to Sapphire.

Address: Levent, Eski Büyükdere Cad. No: 1 D: 1

Operating hours: 10 am to 10 pm

Phone #: +90 212 268 8080

Website: https://www.istanbulsapphire.com/#

Cost (in local currency): 28 TL

Suggested arrival time & duration: For truly spectacular views, head up half an hour before sunset. This way you will see Istanbul at the best of times. Pick a clear day. One to two hours should be ample time for the viewing deck, but more to check out the mall.

6 BEST ISTANBUL EXPERIENCES FOR DAY THREE

Once you've experienced the major highlights in Istanbul, it's time to experience the smaller delights which make life here so incredibly unique.

Here are the best experiences to be had in the city on your final day.

Visit the Spice Bazaar (Mısır Çarşısı) *EMINÖNÜ*

Also known as the Egyptian Bazaar, a visit to this place is a day well spent. Pick up spices, nuts, dried fruit, Coffees and Turkish delights for loved ones at home.

Website: www.misircarsisi.org *(click upper right for English)*

Go to a whirling dervish show

The Mevlevi of whirling dervishes is a show that takes place at least twice a month.

Website: http://www.galatamevlevihanesimuzesi.gov.tr

Ride the red street car *BEYOGLU*

It is nearly impossible to hitch a taxi ride through the crowds in Istanbul, which is why the Red Street Cars are the best alternative –they also add a bit of adventure to your journey!

Walk across the Galata Bridge *GALATA*

The views of Istanbul from this bridge are spectacular, making for pleasant walks in summer.

Cruise down the Bosphorus *BOSPHORUS*

The Bosphorus is one of the largest waterways in the world, taking a boat tour down this magical lane will give you a glimpse of several historic sites such as the Rumeli Ruins and the Maiden's Tower. Take a cheap commuter ferry instead of the expensive tourist boat, and you'll save a bucket-load of liras.

Try some baklava

This delectable sticky and very sweet pastry is covered in nuts and smothered in a honey-like syrup. You'll find it on sale in almost every food stall in town.

Drink Ayran

This is a must try local drink made from frozen yogurt and salts. It may look a bit thick but it goes down easy and is an ideal accompaniment to spicy Turkish food.

Take in the view from Galata Tower *GALATA*

A view of Istanbul from up here is picture perfect! The dramatically pointed roofs of the palaces and mosques are an architectural wonder. One of the city's best sunset spot of all.

Dine at the Hamdi Restaurant *EMINÖNÜ*

The Hamdi is a great place to wine and dine while overlooking some of the most visited buildings in Istanbul such as the Süleymaniye Mosque, Rüstempaşa Mosque and the Galata Tower.

Website: http://hamdi.com.tr/

Catch a show at the Hodjapasha Dance Theatre *SIRKECI*

Come watch a belly-dancing or theatrical show at Istanbul's most revered performance theatre.

Website: http://www.hodjapasha.com/en/

Visit the Chora Church *FATIH*

One of the most splendid churches in Istanbul. The interior is a masterpiece of recreated biblical scenes. A few hours spent here are heavenly!

Website: http://kariye.muze.gov.tr/

The Valens Aqueducts *FATIH*

Historically, this was the first water construction built by the Romans for Constantinople. A guided tour of this place will take you on an informative walk through the city's water system history.

7 AN EXCITING NIGHT OF ENTERTAINMENT IN ISTANBUL

A party lover's delight, the city of Istanbul has an eclectic, young and enthusiastic nightlife. As the sun sets in this old Turkish hub, the energy rises up a notch, and the city marvelously displays its youthful bohemian persona. The nightlife here is as diverse and colorful as its beloved tourist hot-spots. Whether you are looking for a raging nightclub, cozy roof terrace bar or a buzzing concert center, you're bound to find the right Istanbul nightlife spot to suit your tastes.

For your reference, do note our budget guide:

Budget $ -average price for drinks is about 20TL

Mid-range $$ - average price for cocktails come up to about 35TL

Luxe $$$ - expect to spend 50TL for a cocktail here

Each listing begins with the name of the district it is located in for easy planning.

BEYOGLU: U2 Istanbul Irish Pub -A small and cozy bar with genuine world-class beers

$

Drawing hordes of nocturnal partygoers every night, Beyoglu's U2 Istanbul Irish Pub is arguably the hottest and most beloved bar in all of Istanbul. Enjoyed for its cozy vibes and impressive collection of drinks, this trendy Irish pub is a hit with people who love to unwind with a few pints of Guinness. In addition to Guinness, the pub also has more than fifty varieties of beer, including Beck's, Weisse Original, Schneider, Aecht Schlenkerla Rauchbier, Amstel, and Brooklyn Brown Ale.

Additional information

> Address: Sht. Muhtar Mh., Bekar Sk No.21, Beyoglu
>
> Contact number: +90 212 243 4045
>
> Website: http://u2istanbulirishpub.com/irish-pub-in-istanbul-1/
>
> Opening hours: 5 pm to 3 am from Tuesday to Sunday

GALATA: Nardis Jazz Club - A laid-back joint with awesome live jazz music

$$

Looking for an intimate place with wooden floors, brick walls, and soothing jazz music? Tucked away in a historical Turkish district, this jazz bar is indeed one of the most overlooked gems in Istanbul. Named after one of Miles Davis's tracks, this lovely jazz joint plays fine tunes from Turkish jazz luminaries, gifted amateurs and even renowned international artists like Ibrahim Ferrer, Benny Golson and Wynton Marsalis. What's more, the venue has a terrific atmosphere, with superb sound design and exceptional interior lighting effects.

Additional information

>Address: Galata Kulesi Sk. No:8

>Contact number: +90 212 244 6327

>Website: http://nardisjazz.com/

>Opening hours: 8 pm to 1:30 am

BESIKTAS: Anjelique - The most elegant and exclusive club in town

$$$

No list of the best nightspots in Istanbul is complete without the inclusion of Anjelique. One of the most upscale and chic clubs in the city, Anjelique has attracted many world-famous DJs, such as Timo Maas, David Morales, and Boy George. Famed for its ultra-deluxe setting, this waterfront club has plenty of dancing space within its 3-floor venue, even when it is jam packed with the city's brightest celebrities. Plus, it offers great views of the Bosphorus.

Additional information

>Address: Mualim Naci Cad. Salhane Sk. No.10. , Istanbul, Turkey
>
>Contact number: +90 212 287 5641
>
>Website: http://www.anjelique.com.tr/english/
>
>Opening hours: 6 pm to 4 am daily

BEYOGLU: Babylon - Live music at its best

$$

Looking for amped live music in Istanbul? The Babylon is a celebrated multi-performance venue that is packed with diverse musical acts that range from electronic, indie and rock to reggae and jazz. As one of the most sought-after music clubs in the region, Babylon's stage has been graced by several high-caliber musicians, such as Nouvelle Vague, Ed Hardcourt, James Walsh, Stereoland, and Patti Smith.

Additional information

>Address: 3 Sehbender Sokak, Beyoglu
>
>Contact number: +90 212 292 7368

Website: http://babylon.com.tr/en/venues/babylon-istanbul

Opening hours: Schedules vary, depending on the artists. Refer to website, for more information about its schedule and performing artists

ISTIKLAL CADDESI: 360 - A zesty club with a bunch of astounding offers & top sundowner spot

$$

For a wild and heavy dose of nightlife adventure in Istanbul, make it a point to drop by 360. A world-class rooftop restaurant by day, the 360 club shifts gears when the sun goes in Istanbul, making a stylish and desired venue at night. Here, partyholics are with treated non-stop partying as well as live performances from fabulous acts like Martin Solveif and Felix Da Housecat. Not to mention, the venue has an eye-catching modernistic interior design and offers fascinating views of the Sea of Marmara, Golden Horn, and the Bosphorus. Best of all, the venue has a decent selection of delightful wines, cocktails, and spirits.

Additional information

Address: Floor 8, Misir Apartment, 163 Istiklal Caddesi

Contact number: +90 212 251 1042

Website: http://www.360istanbul.com/

Opening hours: 12 pm to 2 am from Monday to Friday, and 12 pm to 4 am on weekends

BEYOGLU: Jolly Joker - A loud and proud indie venue

$

If ritzy clubs aren't your cup of tea, you can avoid all the perfumed crowd at this loud rock, folk and indie venue. An anchor in Istanbul's music scene, the boisterous Jolly Joker features the hottest indie acts and local groups in Turkey.

Additional information:

>Address: 22 Balo Sokak, Beyoglu, Istanbul, Turkey

>Contact number: +90 212 249 0749

>Website: http://www.jjistanbul.com/

Opening hours: 10 pm onwards from Wednesday to Sunday

8 FLAVORS OF THE LOCAL CUISINE

Istanbul is a food lover's paradise and brimming with exceptional epicurean delights, from $2 kebabs served hot off a street-stall to lavish Eastern meals offered by some of the most luxe restaurants in town. The city is awash with phenomenal 'hidden secrets' just itching to be discovered. The best places to eat? The one you never hear or read about, but discover on your own...

Of all the impossibly delectable treats in Istanbul, these are the best ones to look out for:

Çiğköfte

Of all the wraps to try in the city, this is the one you really ought to try, most especially because you'll be hard pressed to find it outside of turkey. Similar to steak tartare, Çiğköfte is a mix of raw minced lamb (sometimes beef), mixed with half a dozen spices, onions and chili pepper. The mixture is massaged by hand for hours, in a process which is said to 'cook' the meat. Spread over a flat pita bread and accompanied by salad and a tangy sauce, this is a very unique, and rather ancient, Turkish recipe to savor.

Simit

Simit is Istanbul's most crowd-pleasing hard-bread, openly sold on the streets and at the local bakeries. The crumbly, ring-shaped carb snack is encrusted with sesame or sunflower seeds, varying from borough to borough within the city. It is served best while still hot during breakfast but can also be a "grab and go" kind of snack. Enjoy it with either a cup of Turkish tea, fruit preserves or cheese. If you've ever had Italian *taralli* then you'll recognize these yummy treats.

Mezes

Mezes are mouthwatering appetizers that can be traced back to the former Ottoman Empire cuisines of the Balkan, Mediterranean, and the Middle East. Mezes are presented in small dishes with different varieties to choose from; among the most common being grilled eggplants and yoghurt, chili tomatoes, olives, chick-pea puree (hummus) and marinated feta cheese. Grab a piece of toasted bread and dive right in.

Lahmacun

Turkey's version of pizza (called pides) are renowned for being both delicious and filling, yet their smaller and much thinner cousin, the lahmacun, is actually one of the best snacks you could have. Seed for a dollar or two in every restaurant, it is THE perfect fresh lunch meal for small eaters.

Hamsi

The arrival of fall means one thing in Istanbul, *hamsi*. No visit to this city is complete prior to indulging in one hamsi or two, that's if you can help it! These are Turkish anchovies caught along the Black Sea's coast, deliciously prepared in several ways, most often deep fried and served with a wedge of lemon. Visitors can enjoy hamsi fillets wrapped around a thick bed of rice with herbs and pine nuts, or pressed around a black olive and then baked in the oven.

Köfte

The Turkish meatball comes in 1010 different variants all over Turkey, most of which are also offered in Istanbul. You can have them as fillings in wraps or on a plate with a side serve of salad and hummus, a chick-pea puree. Restaurants and street-stalls which specialize in offering only this dish are called *Köftecisi*.

Hunkar Begendi

Hunkar Begendi, meaning "The sultans liked it", is a traditional Turkish stew made with chucks of lamb and about a dozen different Middle Eastern spices. As is common with most Turkish dishes, hunkar begendi is served with smoked eggplant, cheese and béchamel sauce. The diced meat chunks are very inviting, and served hot with crusty bread or rice on the side.

Tavuk Gogsu

Temptation is everywhere in Istanbul, beckoning you to indulge yourself in all its delights. Sweets play a key role in Turkish cuisine culture in general and are sold at affordable prices all over Istanbul. Tavuk Gogsu is a unique type of Turkish pudding made with chicken meat; the breasts are softened through intense pounding until they are powdery. The mixture is then thickened with milk and sugar and a sprinkle of cinnamon is added on top for flavor. This treat is served best in summer with a scoop of ice cream. A chicken dessert may sound totally strange, we know, but trust us that this is one dish to be tried!

Kokoreç

Yet another dish said to be an 'acquired taste', Kokorec is a wrap filled with coal roasted lamb intestines wrapped around dubious bits and bobs of offal. Sound appetizing? Hmmm…actually, Kokorec may not sounds delectable but tastes rather delicious. If you're feeling a bit adventurous, look out for this on a restaurant menu and go for gold!

Mantı

These delectable pockets of yumminess are Turkey's answer to the Italian tortellini, and you'll find them served either boiled or fried, and filled with boiled meat marinated in many spices. The most delectable variant comes with a dollop of both spicy tomato sauce and tangy yoghurt. Absolutely mouthwatering!

Our recommended food tour agency:

Culinary Backstreets Food Tours & Cooking Classes

Travel off the beaten path to local markets and discover culinary gems with the Culinary Backstreets team. Munch your way through Istanbul's history while gaining chef insights along the way. Choose from traditional nights of food and culture, comprehensive and hands-on cooking classes and walking & eating tours way off the tourist beaten path. Tour prices range from $75 to $125 per person.

http://www.culinarybackstreets.com/culinary-walks/istanbul/

9 DINING IN ISTANBUL

From hostels to boutique hotels and five-star Now that you're well versed in the wonderful culinary exploits of this amazing city, it's time to take your taste-buds on a feasting tour de force. Where should you go to taste some of the incredible specialties for which this city is so renowned?

Right here!

Budget-friendly restaurants – Where lunch for 2 people should not cost more than 50 TL

Ortaklar Restaurant SULTANAHMET

One of Sultanahmet's best 'cheap and cheerful' options, the Ortaklar serves up no fuss but tasty Turkish fare at very reasonable prices. You'll find this place along the street which runs on the southern end of the Blue Mosque.

Peykhane Street 27, Sultanahmet

+ 90 212 517 6198

Sultanahmet Buhara Kebab House - SULTANAHMET

When it comes to kebabs, very few restaurants in the country are as good as the Sultanahmet Buhara Kebab House. Apart from its exceptional kebab, the restaurant also serves a slew of other Turkish goodies, including garlic lamb, chicken shish kabob, yogurt lamb, iskander kabob, smoked eggplant, and a whole lot more.

Alemdar Mahallesi, Nur-u Osmaniye Caddesi 5, Sultanahmet

+90 212 513 7799

Tarihi Sultanahmet Köftecisi Selim Usta – SULTANAHMET

15TL for a serving of köfte & an Ayran

This great little hidden gem is close to the Sultanahmet Metro Station and specializes in köfte, the tasty and beloved Turkish meatball. This is said to be Sultanahmet's oldest köftecisi!

Minda Mantı ve Ev Yemekleri, BEYOGLU

Here is another cheap and cheerful eatery which specializes in one dish only: Mantı! Their tomato and yoghurt pasta pockets are the most addictive by far.

Cihangir, Sıraselviler Cd. No:43

+90 212 244 8881

Midrange options – You'll pay about 100 TL for dinner for 2 people

Shadow Café Bar Restaurant - SULTANAHMET

Shadow Restaurant is a very modern establishment which boasts excellent food, fast service and great prices for anything more than a grab-n-go snack. What's more, the bar serves some truly wicked cocktails. Great for a leisurely dinner and good-enough prices to make it a regular spot.

Akbiyik Caddesi number 26, Cankurtaran

+90 542 627 8470

Kumkapi Fener Fish Restaurant - SULTANAHMET

Kumkapi Fener Fish Restaurant is, without a doubt, the best seafood restaurant in the city. Here, you get to feast on a variety of signature seafood dishes, such as spicy salad of fresh-rocket and grilled sea-bass. The combination of top location, great food and lovely ambience makes this an excellent choice for a splurge night out. You'll find this restaurant on the south-western end of Sultanahmet, just one block back from Kennedy Street.

Telliodalar Sokak number 5, Kumkapi

+90 212 516 4002

Imbat Restaurant - SULTANAHMET

If you're looking for a gorgeous dinner with a view you really can't walk past Imbat, one of Istanbul's more up-market restaurants. Aside an array of local specialties, you'll also find a few very good international fusion meals. You'll find this lovely restaurant in the old town centre, just 100 meters from the Gulhane Tram Station.

Hocapasa Mh. Hudavendigar Caddesi number 24, Sirkeci

+90 212 520 7191

Upscale - For that ultimate Istanbul dining splurge, expect to pay 140-200 TL

Mikla - BEYOGLU

For over a decade, Mikla has been in the limelight of the city's flourishing culinary scene. Spearheaded by the famous chef Mehmet Gurs, the restaurant boasts an eclectic menu of sumptuous Turkish meals with Scandinavian touches and flavors. Make it a point to try their best-sellers like the salted and dried beef with pistachio and humus, and grilled Aegean octopus. Get in early for sundowners at the spectacular rooftop bar.

The Mamara Pera, 15 Mesrutiyet Caddesi, Beyoglu

+90 212 293 5656

Nicole Restaurant - BEYOGLU

One of the most romantic places to dine in Istanbul, Nicole Restaurant beckons couples, honeymooners and luxurious travelers with its sophisticated style and romantic ambiance. Furthermore, dining here is a true gastronomical experience, with a menu which fuses local and international flavors.

Bogazkesen Cad. Tomtom Kaptak Sk, Beyoglu

+ 90 212 292 4467

Gile Restaurant - BESIKTAS

Gile Restaurant is an innovative, elegant and fine-DINING restaurant renowned for its creativity. The head chef at Giles loves to infuse old classics with eccentric twists, offering an array of degustation menus and wine pairings, to suit even the fussiest connoisseur.

Sair Nedim Caddesi, Akaretler Sive Evleri, Akaratler

+90 212 327 1166

10 ISTANBUL ACCOMMODATION GUIDE

From hostels to boutique hotels and five-star resorts, the city of Istanbul offers an endless selection of accommodations options. Whether you are looking for modern simplicity, budget accommodations or old-fashioned splendor, there is indeed a spot that perfectly suits your taste and budget. But with so many options available, how do you choose the best one for your visit? Here is a list of some of the most recommended accommodations in the Turkish capital. Please do note that prices quoted are for high tourist summer season (June-August), and are subject to change.

Insider's Tip: Istanbul is renowned for its high concentration of marvelous mosques, which are found in every suburb of the city. Although the sunrise call to prayer is both mesmerizing and enchanting, it can also be quite startling to first-time visitors. Pack some ear-plugs if you wish to sleep in!

Budget Hotels

Hanedan Hotel- *SULTANAHMET*

175 TL for double room

In spite of being operated by a quartet of friends, the Hanedan Hotel has a very family and friendly feel about it. In addition, it has gorgeous modern interior decorations that blend perfectly with Ottoman flourishes. As for the rooms, each one comes with air-conditioning and has polished wooden floors. A great low-key choice for budget conscious travelers who want to stay in Sultanahmet.

Akbiyik Caddesi, Adliye Sokak 3, Cankurtaran

+90 212 516 4869

http://hanedanhotel.com

World House Hostel - *GALATA*

190 TL for double room

Nestled dramatically on the cobbled and steep Galipdede Caddesi, the World House Hostel was one of the very first hostels to hit the Golden Horn side. Immaculately clean, bright and light, this functional hostel thrives on providing the most affordable dorm beds in the city.

Galipdede Caddesi, Beyoglu

+90 212 293 5520

http://www.worldhouseistanbul.com

Tulip Guesthouse – *SULTANAHMET*

145 TL for a double room

The Tulip Guesthouse is, by no means, a world-class hotel with exquisite decorations and deluxe amenities. Still, it's been a favorite among foreign travelers due to its affordable rates and clean rooms. Plus, it has a breakfast room where guest can enjoy spectacular views of the sea. Family run and loved, it's one of Old Town's most revered guesthouses.

> Akbiyik Caddesi Terbiyik Sokak number19, Sultanahmet
>
> +90 212 517 6509
>
> http://www.tulipguesthouse.com/

Insider's Tip: Travelling to Istanbul on a tight budget? Then consider finding accommodation in one of the outer suburbs. As long as you are well connected by either dolmus or Metro (or a combination of the two) adding even a 20-minute ride in and out of the historic centre can seriously reduce your accommodation cost. Check out AirBnB's selection in the suburbs over the Galata Bridge and you can find great digs for as little as USD 20.

Midrange Hotels

Osmanhan Hotel – *SULTANAHMET*

350 TL for double room

Located right at the heart of Istanbul's old city, the Osmanhan Hotel is just a few minutes' walk from Topkapi Palace, Hagia Sofia and the Blue Mosque. The rooms are spacious yet cozy, well-appointed and very well serviced. The gorgeous rooftop terrace at this hotel is ideal for a delightful breakfast with a breathtaking view. Do note that this hotel is not wheelchair accessible.

> Akbiyik Cad. Cetinkaya Sok. Number 1, Sultanahmet
>
> +90 212 458 7702
>
> http://www.osmanhanhotel.com/

Istanbul Hotel Uyan - *SULTANAHMET*

315 TL for double room

As far as location, no other hotel in the city can top the Istanbul Hotel Uyan. Located in-between the Blue Mosque and Hagia Sophia, the Istanbul Hotel Uyan is a lovely hotel that gives you easy access to the city's prized sights and tourist darlings. Besides its superlative location, the hotel offers premium service and excellent amenities, making it one of the best choices in its price range.

> Utangac Sokak No 25, Sultanahmet

+90 212 516 4892

https://www.uyanhotel.com/

Midtown Hotel – *TAKSIM*

345 TL for double room

Nestled right at the heart of modern Istanbul, this four-star hotel is a great base for shopping addicts and foodies, as well as those who like to be close to the nighttime action. It certainly doesn't hurt that what you get for the price, are full western amenities and comfort, along with exceptional service.

> Lamartin Cad. Number 13 Taksim, Beyoglu, Istanbul, Turkey
>
> +90 212 361 6767
>
> http://www.midtown-hotel.com/

Luxury & Boutique Hotels

Hotel Ibrahim Pasha - *SULTANAHMET*

345 TL for double room

Istanbul's historic centre is actually brimming with innumerable boutique hotels, most of which have been created from private luxury homes. The Ibrahim Pasha Hotel is one such treasure. Small, ultra-deluxe and cozy as can be is just steps from the Blue Mosque and room rates include a delectable continental breakfast.

>Terzihane Sokak 5, Sultanahmet

>+90 212 518 0394

>http://www.ibrahimpasha.com/

Insider's Tip: Boutique hotels in Istanbul are usually family owned, so although they offer an exceptionally luxe stay, they usually cost half as much as a standard, 4* hotel.

Grand Hyatt Istanbul - *BEYOGLU*

575 TL for double room

The Hyatt group of hotels are renowned for their class and top-notch service and amenities. The Istanbul branch is no different. A top choice in its price range, the Grand Hyatt Istanbul boasts a superlative location and all the mod-cons you'd expect of a 5* hotel, with the added opulence of an Ottoman-ear inspired architecture.

>Taskisla Cad. 1 Taksim, Beyoglu

>+90 212 368 1234

>http://istanbul.grand.hyatt.com/en/hotel/home.html

Super Deluxe Splurge

Four Seasons Istanbul at the Bosphorus - *BESIKTAS*

7760 TL for a double room

Housed in a dazzling Ottoman palace, the Four Seasons Istanbul at the Bosphorus is probably the most alluring and opulent hotel in the entire city, with room rates to match. Not only does this 6* hotel feature outstanding architecture, but it also showcases its opulent luxury in every detail. To make your stay even more pleasurable, the hotel has a cluster of facilities, including spa facilities, indoor pool, heated outdoor pool, and many more. If you've ever wanted to experience life as a Sultan, now's your chance!

> Ciragan Cad. number 28, Besiktas, Istanbul, Turkey
>
> +90 212 381 4000
>
> http://www.fourseasons.com/bosphorus/

11 ISTANBUL TRAVEL ESSENTIALS

Istanbul is a great place to visit with exceptionally warm and friendly locals. To ensure you have a pleasant journey while in the city, it's important to know which currency to use, how to make phone calls, their standard meal times etc.

Here is a list of a few essentials that may come in handy:

Currency

The *Yeni Türk Lirası* (YTL, TL, or New Turkish Lira) is the official currency used in Istanbul. Be sure to check the Turkish Central Bank for current exchange rates; exchange offices are located at the Airport close to the Arrivals Terminals and you'll find many more in the historic centre of town. You will need to have cash on you during your stay in Istanbul as there are certain hotels and restaurants that don't accept credit cards. There are ATMs placed throughout Istanbul; withdraw money in a public area, for optimum safety.

Phone Calls

Calling an Istanbul landline from the United States/Canada:

Dial **011** (exit code) followed by **90** (country code for Turkey) then **212 (Europe side) or 216 (Asia side)** (Istanbul area codes) before finally dialing the **local number**.

011 + 90 + 212 + local number

Calling Istanbul mobile from the United States/Canada:

Dial **011** (exit code) followed by **90** (country code for Istanbul) then the **mobile number**.

011 + 90 + local number

Calling Istanbul landline from Europe/Globally:

Dial **00** followed by **90** (country code for Turkey) then **212 (Europe side) or 216 (Asia side)** (Istanbul area codes) before finally dialing the **local number**.

00 + 90 + 212 + local number

Calling Istanbul mobile from Europe/Globally:

Dial **0 + 90 +5** then the **mobile number**.

0 + 90 +5 + local number

When calling from Istanbul to another country you will simply dial the international prefix (00) followed by the code of the country you are calling.

00 + country code + area code + local number

Local calls within Turkey

Landline: **Dial 0 + 212 (or 216 for Asia side) + local number**

Mobile: **Dial +90 + mobile number**

Standard Meal Times

The Turks eat when they're hungry, and pay no mind to time but breakfast is typically from 6am to 11am. Lunch is between 12noon and 2pm. Dinner is from 9pm until late.

Business hours:

Public establishments, private businesses and banks in Istanbul are open for business from 8:30am to 6pm daily, with a lunch break around 1:30pm. Official opening hours for shops are Monday to Saturday 9am-6pm. In summer, many shops, especially those in tourist areas, remain open until around 9pm. Museums are typically open from 9:30am to 5pm, Mon-Sat.

Key Closure Days:

Like in any other country, official and religious public holidays are celebrated with great joy. Most sightseeing spots are closed on Mondays, or only open until 1pm during Religious Holidays. The official holidays are, New Year's Eve 1 January, The Feast of Ramadan in March, The Feast of Sacrifice in April, Victory Day on the 30th of August and Republic Holiday on the 29th of October.

12 TURKISH LANGUAGE ESSENTIALS

Greetings & Conversation

Hello.

Merhaba.

(*mehr hah bah*)

How are you? (polite/plural)

Nasılsınız?

(*na suhl suhn uhz*)

Fine, thank you.

İyiyim, teşekkürler.

(*ee yee yeem teh shek ür lerr*)

What is your name? (polite)

Adınız nedir?

(*ad uhn uhz ne deer*)

My name is _____ .

Adım _____ .

(*Ad uhm* ____ .)

or

Benim adım ____ .

(*Benn im ad uhm* ____ .)

Benim emphasizes that the name is yours.

Nice to meet you.

Memnun oldum.

(*mem noon oll doom*)

Please.

Lütfen.

(*Luet fen*)

Thank you.

Teşekkür ederim.

(*teh shek uer eh der eem*)

You're welcome.

Bir şey değil.

(*bir shey de yeel*)

I don't understand.

Anlamıyorum

(*An-la-muh-yoor-uhm*),

or

I didn't understand

Anlamadım

(*An la ma duhm*)

Yes.

Evet.

(*eh vet*)

No.

Hayır.

(*Hah yuhr*)

I'm sorry.

Pardon.

(*Par don*)

Goodbye (polite/plural, used by the person leaving)

Hoşçakalın.

(*Hosh cha kaluhn*)

Good morning.

Günaydın.

(*Guen eye duhn*)

Good evening.

İyi akşamlar.

(*e yee ak sham lar*)

Helpful Phrases in Emergencies

Where is the toilet?

Tuvalet nerede?

(*Too va let ner eh de?*)

Is there any ...?

... var mı?

(*var Muh*)

Help!

İmdat!

(*Im Daht!*)

Doctor

doktor

(*dok tor*)

Leave me alone.

Beni yalnız bırak.

(*beh nee yahl nuz bu rahk*)

Police!

Polis!

(*poh lees*)

I need your help.

Yardımınıza ihtiyacım var.

(*yahr duh muh nuh zah eeh tee yah juhm vahr*)

It's an emergency.

Acil durum.

(*ah jeel doo room*)

I'm lost.

Kayboldum.

(*kahy bohl doom*)

I lost my wallet.

Cüzdanımı kaybettim.

(*jooz dah nuh muh kahy beht teem*)

I'm sick.

Hastayım.

(*hahs tah yuhm*)

Can I use your phone?

Telefonunuzu kullanabilir miyim?

(*teh leh foh noo noo zoo kool lah nah bee leer mee yeem*)

Numbers

1 bir

(*beer*)

2 iki

(*icki*)

3 üç

(*uech*)

4 dört

(*dirt*)

5 beş

(*besh*)

6 altı

(*altuh*)

7 yedi

(*yedi*)

8 sekiz

(*sekiz*)

9 dokuz

(*dokuz*)

10 on

(*on*)

Transportation

Which bus?

hangi otobüs

(*hangee auto boos*)

How much is a ticket to _____?

_____'a bir bilet kaç para?

(___ *ah beer bee leht kach pah rah*)

One ticket to _____, please.

_____'a bir bilet lütfen.

(___ *ah beer bee leht loot fehn*)

Where does this train/bus go?

Bu tren/otobüs nereye gider?

(*boo tee rehn/oh toh boos neh reh yeh gee dehr*)

Where is the train/bus to _____?

_____'a giden tren/otobüs nerede?

(___ *ah gee dehn tee rehn/oh toh boos neh reh deh*)

Does this train/bus stop in _____?

Bu tren/otobüs _____'da durur mu?

(*boo tee rehn/oh toh boos ___ dah doo roor moo*)

Where?

(place) nerede?

(*nar edeh*)

(direction) nereye?

(*nar eyeh*)

Left sol

(*sole*)

Right sağ

(*saa*)

Straight düz

(*dooz*)

Here burada

(*bur ah da*)

Shopping

How much (money)?

kaç para?

(*koch pa rah*)

Cheap

ucuz

(*oo juuz*)

Expensive

pahalı

(*pahaluh*)

Black

Siyah

(*see yah*)

White

Ak

(*ak*)

Yellow

Sarı

(*saa rıh*)

Blue

Mavi

(*mao vee*)

Navy

Lacivert

(*la jee vert*)

Green

Yeşil

(*yea sheal*)

Red

Kızıl

(*khızıl*)

Pink

Pembe

(*pam bhe*)

Orange

Turuncu

(*too roon joo*)

Purple

Mor

(*more*)

Brown

Kahverengi

(*kaah ve rengi*)

Food & Dining

Waiter, excuse me.

bakar mısınız?

(*ba kar mis in izz*)

Menu/price list

Menü / fiyat listesi

(*fee yot lis tesi*)

Bill

hesap (*he sap*)

May I have some _____?

Biraz _____ alabilir miyim?

(*bee raaz ___ ah lah bee leer mee yeem*)

Coffee

kahve

(*kaahh veh*)

Tea (*drink*)

çay

(*chaay*)

Juice

meyve suyu

(*may veh soo yoo*)

Carbonated water

soda

(*soh dah*)

Water

su

(*soo*)

Beer

Bira

(*bee rah*)

Red/white wine

kırmızı/beyaz şarap

(*kuhr muh zuh/beh yaaz shaa raap*)

Chicken

tavuk

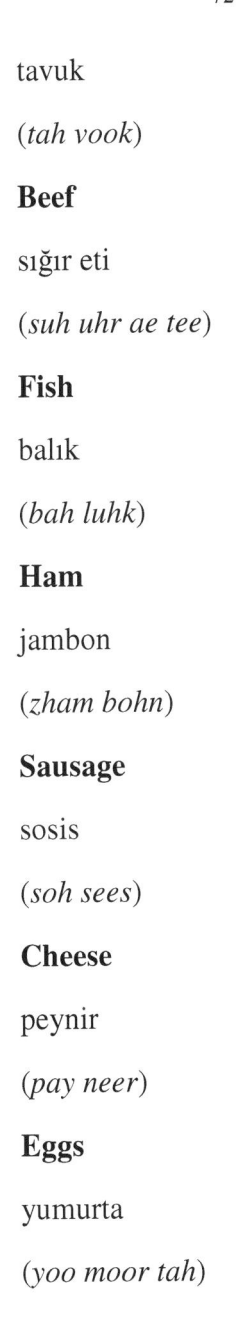

(*tah vook*)

Beef

sığır eti

(*suh uhr ae tee*)

Fish

balık

(*bah luhk*)

Ham

jambon

(*zham bohn*)

Sausage

sosis

(*soh sees*)

Cheese

peynir

(*pay neer*)

Eggs

yumurta

(*yoo moor tah*)

Salad

salata

(*sah lah tah*)

Fresh vegetables

taze sebze

(*(tah zeh) sehb zeh*)

Fresh fruit

(taze) meyve

(*(tah zeh) may veh*)

Bread

ekmek

(*ehk mehk*)

Important Signs & Their Meanings

AÇIK Open

KAPALI Closed

GİRİŞ Entrance

ÇIKIŞ Exit

İTİNİZ Push

ÇEKİNİZ Pull

TUVALET / WC Toilet

BAY Men

BAYAN Women

YASAKTIR Forbidden

13 CONCLUSION

With its awe-inspiring historical sites and intriguing vibe, it's no wonder the city of Istanbul has become a darling to millions of travelers from all over the world. From soothing Turkish baths and hectic aromatic bazaars to the towering skyscrapers, this otherworldly haven has a mixture of experiences that can keep you entertained for days or even weeks on end. Despite its astounding size and incredible variety of attractions, you can still experience the true essence of this glorious ancient in less than a week. Just take note of the pointers shared in this guide, and you will undoubtedly have the time of your life in Istanbul.

Elveda!

Printed in Great Britain
by Amazon